OUT OF THE DARKNESS

OUT OF THE DARKNESS

THE MYSTERY AND MAJESTY OF GOD'S CREATION

CODY CARLSON

To Micah, Anna, Matthew, Will, J.D., and Jennifer—
may you know the love that God has for you.

Out of the Darkness: The Mystery and Majesty of God's Creation
Copyright © 1998 by Cody Carlson
Published by Baxter Press

ISBN: 1-888237-13-9

Note: The translation of the Bible used in this book is the New
International Version.

Cover design by John Gilmore

Acknowledgements

This book would not have been possible without the help of many individuals who shared their knowledge, their love, and their support. Many thanks. . .

. . . to Mom and Dad for showing and teaching me about life.

. . . to my wife, Barbara, for her endless patience and love, and for her photographs which make this book complete.

. . . to John and Tanya, Oscar and Joan, Michael and Tracy, Bill Meador, Buddy Miles, and the Wynn family for letting me walk across their land in my quest for pictures.

. . . to Bruce Roberts and Steve Whitaker for sharing their knowledge and love of God's creation with me.

. . . to Carol Bronick for sharing her roof and lessons of the mission.

. . . to Don Sapaugh for believing in this book and getting the process started to create it.

. . . to Pat Springle for helping in many aspects of that process.

. . . to Mike Myers, Reagan Lambert, Dennis Connor, Ralph Stewart, Dal Shealy, and many others with the Fellowship of Christian Athletes for their friendship, interest, and support.

. . . and to the friends who have opened their homes and their lives to me, and for their company that made journeys, which would have been long and lonely, much more enjoyable.

Photos by Barbara Carlson pp. 104, 173, 185, 186, 188, 192, 198, 202

Table of Contents

Introduction

I've always loved wild places. My thoughts are full of fading memories of family camping and fishing trips when I was a little boy. The images come in fragments: a rock skipping across a still lake, sand in my eggs at breakfast, a big bass slashing at a topwater lure, ducks on a log, a rabbit running to cover. . . . The memories make me smile even today. My experiences left me with lasting impressions and wide-eyed wonder.

My father often went hunting when I was very small, and I begged to go along. I cried bitter tears of disappointment when I was left behind with my mother and my sister. Dad always returned with wonderful stories of strange creatures he had seen. I listened to every word. . . and then asked him to tell the stories again!

Finally, I was old enough to go along, to walk with my Dad and crunch dried leaves under our feet next to the rivers and under the trees. Everything fascinated me! My Dad taught me how to hunt and fish, and he taught me how to identify particular birds by the angle of their wings, the shape of their beaks, and the slight variations in the color of their feathers. Dad showed me how to track animals in the wet bottomland or the dry, dusty desert.

Over the years, my sense of wonder at the natural world hasn't dimmed a bit. In fact, as my knowledge has grown, my wonder has multiplied. I've learned to appreciate wildlife in new ways. In my early years, it was a source of great pride to have a stringer of fish so long that I couldn't possibly clean and eat all of them. Later I caught just as many, but most went back into the water to grow and fight again. And hunting with a gun has largely been replaced with hunting with a camera. Photography enables me to appreciate nature in fresh, new ways, and it challenges me to see more fully—and more clearly—than ever before.

My first attempts to capture nature on film frustrated me. I could see the image, but I couldn't make the picture match my mind's vision of it. Part of my problem was education. To tell the truth, the problem was playing hooky. I didn't want to sit and read about the intricacies of photography when I could be outside enjoying the scenery and the animals! My other problem was my equipment. The camera I used probably was discarded by Matthew Brady in about 1868! Not quite good enough to meet my expectations in photography!

When I received my first bonus check from the Houston Oilers, I used it to buy a new camera and lenses with all the bells and whistles, and I made the supreme sacrifice (at least for me!). I spent hours in my apartment reading book after book on nature photography by artists like Thomas Mangelson, Art Wolfe, David Muench, Leonard Rue, Stephen Kirkpatrick, Wyman Meinzer, and Lawrence Parent. I was inspired by their artistry, and I dreamed of emulating them.

When I wasn't reading and studying about photography, I wandered around out in the woods and scrub brush of central Texas to try my newly acquired knowledge on some real, live critters. To my surprise and delight, some of these pictures turned out quite good. I was hooked!

As my confidence grew, I traveled to new places and saw animals I'd never seen before. And I met some remarkable people. For eight years, I drove and paddled and flew all over the place. One day, I asked myself a question I should have asked long before: "Why?" Why was I wandering around in the woods away from my beautiful wife? Why did I spend hours figuring out how to take the "perfect" picture of an owl, a squirrel, or a waterfall? As I struggled with these questions, my desire began to grow for others to enjoy the creatures and scenery that I had been fortunate enough to see. A new question slowly formed in my mind: "What is it that I really want to communicate to people?" Through prayer—and the prodding of some good friends—I realized that it wasn't just the pictures that I wanted to share. It was something much deeper.

One day as I drove my pickup through the Texas panhandle on a lonely road, I heard the words of a Rich Mullins song:

> And the single hawk bursts into flight and in the
> east the whole
> horizon is in flames
> I feel the thunder in the sky
> I see the sky about to rain
> And I hear the prairies calling out Your name
> > Rich Mullins, "Calling Out Your Name"
> > *The World as Best as I Remember It*, Volume 1

At that moment, I realized my pictures weren't something I had created at all. These were images of some of the creatures and places that call out God's name! They are images of his creation.

This book is not a "how to" on photography, because I'm not qualified to teach those skills. And this is not a systematic study of animal behavior by a board-certified zoologist. That's not me, either. This book expresses my deep appreciation—in fact, my genuine *passion*—for God's creation. I am astounded by the delicate intricacies of a spider's web, the vibrant colors of a wood duck, and the awesome majesty of a mountain at sunset. In his creation God has shown his power, his order, his attention to minute detail. . . and sometimes, his humor! I hope you enjoy these pages, but more than that, I hope you appreciate the Creator a little more as you see his handiwork.

This book is only a fleeting glimpse of God's creative work. Even the most creative eye cannot possibly capture the breadth of his glory. The brush of the most talented painter will never equal the awe-inspiring pageantry of nature, nor will the most ingenious computers ever match the intricate details of the animal and plant kingdoms. The roar of the lion, the speed of the falcon, and the falling of a leaf in autumn sing of the greatness of God.

Ultimately, our appreciation of the created world causes us to reflect on our unique role in it. We are here to observe, to learn, to protect, and to govern, but much more than this, we exist to praise God for his greatness, his love, and his sovereignty over all his works. We accept his many gifts, and we in turn give thanks and seek to serve the Giver.

The heavens declare the glory of God;
the skies proclaim the work of his hands.
Psalm 19:1

In the beginning. . .

. . .God created the heavens and the earth. Now the earth
was formless and empty, darkness was over the surface of
the deep, and the Spirit of God was hovering over the
waters.

And God said, "Let there be light," and there was light. God saw
that the light was good, and he separated the light from the
darkness. God called the light "day," and the darkness he called
"night." And there was evening, and there was morning—the
first day.
And God said, "Let there be an expanse between the waters to
separate water from water." So God made the expanse and
separated the water under the expanse from the water above it.
And it was so. God called the expanse "sky." And there was
evening, and there was morning—the second day.
And God said, "Let the water under the sky be gathered to one
place, and let dry ground appear." And it was so. God called the
dry ground "land," and the gathered waters he called "seas."
And God saw that it was good.

Then God said, "Let the land produce vegetation: seed-bearing plants and trees on the land that bear fruit with seed in it, according to their various kinds." And it was so. The land produced vegetation: plants bearing seed according to their kinds and trees bearing fruit with seed in it according to their kinds. And God saw that it was good. And there was evening, and there was morning—the third day.

And God said, "Let there be lights in the expanse of the sky to separate the day from the night, and let them serve as signs to mark seasons and days and years, and let them be lights in the expanse of the sky to give light on the earth." And it was so. God made two great lights—the greater light to govern the day and the lesser light to govern the night. He also made the stars. God set them in the expanse of the sky to give light on the earth, to govern the day and the night, and to separate light from darkness.

And God saw that it was good. And there was evening, and there was morning—the fourth day.

And God said, "Let the water teem with living creatures, and let birds fly above the earth across the expanse of the sky." So God created the great creatures of the sea and every living and moving thing with which the water teems, according to their kinds, and every winged bird according to its kind. And God saw that it was good. God blessed them and said, "Be fruitful and increase in number and fill the water in the seas, and let the birds increase on the earth." And there was evening, and there was morning—the fifth day.

And God said, "Let the land produce living creatures according to their kinds: livestock, creatures that move along the ground, and wild animals, each according to its kind." And it was so. God made the wild animals according to their kinds, the livestock according to their kinds, and all the creatures that move along the ground according to their kinds. And God saw that it was good.

Then God said, "Let us make man in our image, in our likeness, and let them rule over the fish of the sea and the birds of the air, over the livestock, over all the earth, and over all the creatures that move along the ground."

So God created man in his own image, in the image of God he created him; male and female he created them.

God blessed them and said to them, "Be fruitful and increase in number; fill the earth and subdue it. Rule over the fish of the sea and the birds of the air and over every living creature that moves on the ground."

Then God said, "I give you every seed-bearing plant on the face of the whole earth and every tree that has fruit with seed in it. They will be yours for food. And to all the beasts of the earth and all the birds of the air and all the creatures that move on the ground—everything that has the breath of life in it—I give every green plant for food." And it was so.

And God saw all that he had made, and it was very good. And there was evening, and there was morning—the sixth day.

Thus the heavens and the earth were completed in all their vast array.

By the seventh day God had finished the work he had been doing; so on the seventh day he rested from all his work. And God blessed the seventh day and made it holy, because on it he rested from all the work of creating that he had done.

Genesis 1:1-2:3

Southfields

But ask the animals, and they will teach you,
    or the birds of the air, and they will teach you;
or speak to the earth, and it will teach you,
    or let the fish of the sea inform you.
Which of all these does not know
    that the hand of the Lord has done this?
In his hand is the life of every creature
    and the breath of all mankind.
                Job 12:7-10

In our country the Coastal Plain runs from the falls of navigable rivers to the seashore. In Georgia the plains begin at the fall line at Columbus, Macon, and Augusta; in Texas they reach from the Hill Country and the Piney Woods to the Gulf.

The southfields reveal many different shapes: from rolling hills to cactus barrens, from hayfields to sand dunes. Within these borders, a wide variety of landscapes, plants, and animals thrives. This diversity tells us about a Creator with a marvelous plan, because these shapes contain intricacies which couldn't have evolved from one cell or one particle of cosmic dust. They came from a single, loving, creative, brilliant source—the hand of God.

Daybreak finds white-tailed deer in a hayfield.

The Rattlesnake

Tears streamed down my face as I looked at the motionless bird in my hands. I was eight years old with a BB gun, and my grandmother had told me, "Don't shoot the house wren. It has a nest on the porch." But when the little bird landed on a fence post on the far side of the yard, the temptation proved too great.

That was not the last time I felt remorse over the death of an animal I had killed. To a certain extent, I experience those same emotions every time the challenge of a hunt is over.

A few days after I killed the house wren, tears rolled down my face again as I stared at the dead rattlesnake lying at my feet. I clutched the same BB gun, but this time, I was crying because my prized weapon's barrel was smashed when my father used it to bludgeon the snake. I don't recall ever again shedding a tear at the scene of a rattlesnake's death.

A lot of old-time Texans will tell you, "Leave every gate the way you found it, and kill every rattlesnake you see." Certainly rattlesnakes can be dangerous, but there are a few old Texans who disagree with this adage. Barbara's Pappy tells of the time when he was a youngster helping his father load oats onto a wagon. Pappy looked down from the wagon bed and saw that his father had accidentally stepped on a rattler's tail! It was thrashing from side to side next to his leg! Pappy's father didn't even notice because he was so intent on loading that wagon, so Pappy yelled, "Look out! Rattler!"

His father simply moved his foot and allowed the snake to slither away. Pappy jumped down off the wagon and killed the snake. Later, though, Pappy had second thoughts. He told Barbara, "I should have left that snake for seed. Then we'd have grown rattlers that wouldn't bite!"

It's a rare rattler that doesn't become instantly aggressive when it is startled or threatened. In fact, some of their kind have been known to be dangerous even after they were thought to be dead. My grandfather, Joe, told me that a rattlesnake isn't really dead until the sun goes down. Now that might be just a tall, Texas tale, but my friend, Bruce, probably believes it.

This rattlesnake was found soaking in the warmth of a dirt road. Through the lens, the snake looked a lot closer than he actually was. Each time the angry rattler moved, I peeked out from behind the camera to make sure he remained at a safe distance.

27

Bruce had killed a rattler in a pasture near his hunting camp in south Texas. He picked it up to carry it back to the truck, but the snake's head suddenly moved toward Bruce's arm! Bruce jumped and flung that snake so hard that he separated his shoulder!

Few creatures are the source of more folklore than the rattlesnake, and I don't know many that create such explosive emotions in people. I've spent much of my life in the outdoors, and I feel comfortable encountering almost any animal. But when I stumble upon a rattler, the hairs on the back of my neck stand on end! The buzz of its tail and the evil look in its eyes make my skin crawl! Still. . . my emotions are mixed. Along with the fear is a certain fascination with this mysterious creature. At times, I've been the first in line to kill a menacing rattler, but on other occasions, I've watched others crawl away unharmed. My emotions and my actions are inconsistent, but my beliefs about rattlesnakes are not. I am convinced that the earth would be a little poorer if this animal no longer slithered across its hills and swamps. I'm not sure why God created rattlesnakes. Maybe they are necessary in his creation for the balance of nature. Or maybe the rush of adrenaline we experience when we encounter them lets us know we are alive. . . and vulnerable. That's not a bad lesson to learn.

A savannah sparrow on a spiked perch.

Prickly pear cactus thrive throughout the arid land.

Harris hawk chicks in their nest. Harris hawks often hunt in packs. They are the only hawk known to exhibit this behavior.

Odd things, they say—even their looks—will let the secret out.
C. S. Lewis, *The Lion, The Witch, and the Wardrobe*

Two of the strangest creatures in Texas are the wild turkey and the horned lizard. This tom turkey was very proud of his looks as he strutted for the hens. He was so consumed with passion that he continued his display while I approached and photographed him. Male turkeys can engage in vicious battles, pushing, biting, kicking, and making all sorts of noises. The feathers fly but the birds are rarely seriously injured. I observed a group of five young toms, called "jakes," gang up on an older, bigger tom with his harem of hens. The jakes chased him in and out of the brush, through fields, and over fences, all the while plucking feathers from the beautiful fan-like tail that was the source of his vanity.

The "horney toad," as it is known to most of us, acts as strange as it looks. In the face of danger, it flattens its body and hisses a warning. It may even threaten to bite. If all else fails, some species of horned lizards squirt streams of blood from the corners of their eyes to ward off enemies.

A buck emerges from a veil of fog.

Opposite: Head to head.

Most of us think of deer as perhaps the most peaceful animals in the forest. And they are. . . most of the year. But during the rut, bucks fight to gain dominance over each other to insure their proper place in mating season. They violently push and gouge other bucks to try to dominate them. Hunters eagerly anticipate this period when normally timid bucks throw caution to the wind and boldly defend their territory against any challengers.

I was able to observe this behavior at close range thanks to a friend named Milo. He had worked on a ranch for many years, and when he whistled, the deer came out of the cover of thick brush to eat the corn he offered them. Their natural instinct to fight or flee was overcome by the trust Milo had established with them over many years.

Maybe that's the same thing that happens between us and God. By his patient and persistent love, he earns our trust. Then—and only then—will we overcome our natural instincts to fight or flee and respond in intimacy and thankfulness.

Snow geese.

Opposite: A red-winged
blackbird sings his song on
a spring morning.

Wild lantana.

Green jay.

Be praised for all Your tenderness
        by these works of Your hands
Suns that rise and rains that fall to
        bless and bring to life Your land
        look down upon this winter wheat
        and be glad that You have made
Blue for the sky and the color green
        that fills Your fields
        with praise
                Rich Mullins, "The Color Green"
                A Liturgy, A Legacy, and A Ragamuffin Band

White-tailed deer.

Red-tailed hawk.

Opposite: Tom turkeys gobble during the spring breeding season. A friend of mine looked at this picture, and he said, "You ought to title this one 'Staff Meeting'! It reminds me of some people I worked with." We had a good laugh.

*A green-winged teal glides
to a lake that mirrors the
color of the evening sky.*

Raccoon.

A harrier hawk looks for a meal in the tall grass of a coastal prairie.

Opposite: A cottontail rabbit stretches for the beans of a mesquite tree.

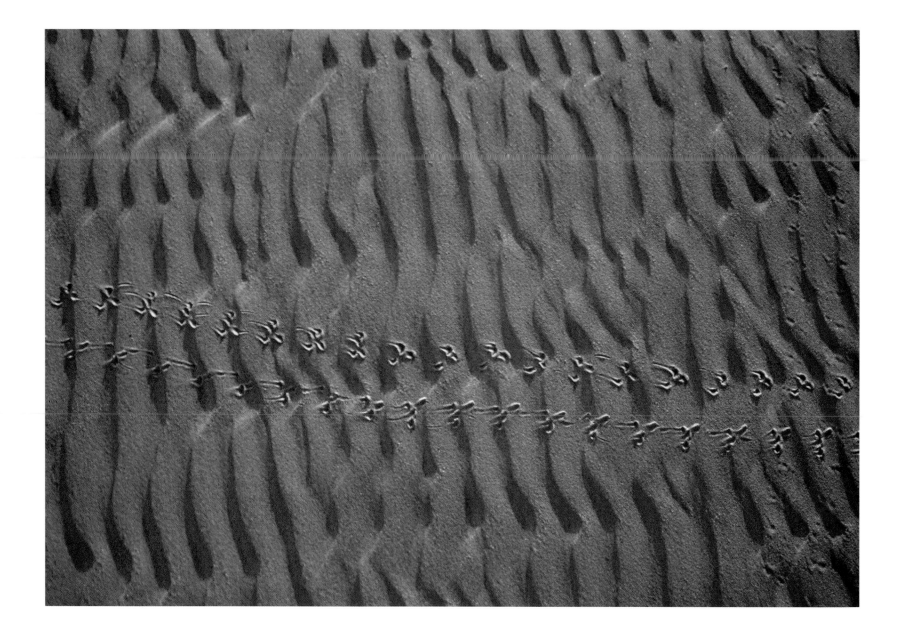

Tracks

Tracks reveal the story of passing creatures. A single set of prints across the sand dunes tells of a lonely journey.

Sometimes we see two sets of tracks. The footprints of a coyote often intermingle with those of a rabbit, leaving evidence of a life-and-death drama played out over the dunes. But blowing sand will soon erase this story.

The tracks we leave behind are a legacy for generations to come. What will we leave? What path will our children follow? It's impossible to cover every misstep, but a commitment to walk a straight path—and honesty about our missteps—is also a path worth following. We talk of changing our nation and even our world, but we need to be sure we change our own tracks first.

> *I will utter hidden things, things from of old—*
> *   what we have heard and known,*
> *   what our fathers have told us.*
> *We will not hide them from their children;*
> *   we will tell the next generation*
> *the praiseworthy deeds of the Lord,*
> *   his power, and the wonders he has done.*
> *   Psalm 78:2b-4*

I was in South Texas when a spring norther suddenly hit. I thought the 40 mph winds would drive even the most diehard springbreakers from the coast, so I decided to venture on south.

When I arrived at the beach, I found torn tents and discarded camping equipment under drifts of sand. These were the only things left by the vacationers. The blowing sand stung the skin and filled every opening in my face and my truck, but I enjoyed watching the shorelife adapt to the harsh conditions. I watched several brown pelicans use the larger-than-normal waves as a windbreak as they ventured into the teeth of the wind.

I took this shot of one of the birds as he crested a wave. He turned back out to sea to catch another wave and slowly made his way up the coast.

Opposite: A diminutive snowy plover stands against strong winds at the surf's edge.

*A Louisiana heron fishes
the shallow water along the
coastline.*

Snowy egret.

Coastal storm.

God's voice thunders in marvelous ways;
    he does great things beyond our understand-
ing.
He says to the snow, "Fall on the earth,"
    and to the rain shower, "Be a mighty down-
pour."

Job 37:5-6

Swamplands

Sunset is clear and dramatic in most landscapes, but in the swamps, evening only finishes darkening the scene. Even in midday, this land is shrouded in a strange twilight. Few of the sun's rays filter through the thatched canopy of leaves, limbs, and moss. In these shadows, time and direction lose their place, and all living things seem to merge into one tangled form, providing a perfect hide-out for the animals. The air is heavy and still, but it is alive with odd sounds of hidden things. As if by magic, a lone creature emerges from the tangle and gives us a glimpse of itself, and then it vanishes as quickly as it appeared.

Swamplands are mysterious places. They are full of intrigue. Swamps have the power to make us marvel and wonder. . . like children all over again.

A dense thicket of moss and trees provides cover for the creatures of the swamp.

A Ray of Light

A tree-lined pass. . . a whistling scream. . . a splash in the flooded timber. A wood duck glides across the water. A shaft of sunlight dodges the trees to shine on the orange eye of a motionless night heron as it hunts in the shallows. A dozen white flashes signal the startled herd of white-tailed deer as they dart through the trees. The haunting call of a barred owl, the hooting laughter of a moorhen, the odd, vibrating roar of a mate-crazed alligator. These animals hide in the dense tangle of the swamp and are seldom seen by outsiders, but if you linger long enough, you'll find an incredible richness of life.

I needed a place to hide, too. It took me a long time to find such a place. I arrived in Houston in 1987 to play football for the Oilers, and I quickly jumped into a frantic routine of blitzes, bruises, media scrutiny, and traffic jams. The city promised to provide everything a young man could want—except peace and solitude.

I had to get away. To think. To pray. I wanted answers. Why is tragedy the most common topic in the news? Why does God allow such suffering? Bad news comes in wave after wave. I got used to it. Sort of. After a while, my spirit was overloaded, and I needed some peace.

We find hope, not in the pursuit of speed and success, but in the kind word of a friend, the loving touch of a spouse, the laughter of a child, or the smile of a stranger. And if we look hard enough, we'll find people who possess a hope that is tested and true: a woman with a thankful heart even though she is alone; a child who smiles even though he is in pain; or a man who has the courage to believe that Almighty God does, after all, know what he's doing.

> *Look at the birds of the air, for they neither*
> *sow nor reap nor gather into barns; yet your*
> *Heavenly Father feeds them. Are you not of more*
> *value than they?*
> *Matthew 6:26*

Not too far from the madding crowd, I sat quietly and watched the creatures of the swamp. I marveled at how God provides for each of them in different ways, and I found hope and peace.

A common egret snatches a dragonfly from the air.

Two alligators cozy up to one another to get some afternoon sun.

Opposite: White ibis sleep in the top of a dead tree.

A Louisiana heron in the flooded timber of the swamp.

Opposite: Black-bellied whistling ducks fly over a marsh in search of a place to land.

What would the world be once bereft
Of wet and of wildness? Let them be left,
O let them be left, wildness and wet:
Long live the weeds and the wilderness yet.
    Gerard Manly Hopkins, *Inversnaid*

A redbud tree blooms in the dense woods.

Opposite: An osprey leaves its perch to fish a bayou.

A young purple gallinule
crosses the water on lily
pads.

Opposite: A tufted titmouse
clutches a nut as it sits on
the branch of a redbud tree.

Gator

I peered through the view finder of my camera lens, waiting. . . waiting. . . waiting for that moment all nature photographers long for but seldom see. This scene was perfect. Good light in the warm morning sun. Great reflections of the lily pads and background. A purple gallinule almost walking on water as it stepped from lily pad to lily pad on its elongated, gangly toes. It wouldn't be long now.

My anticipation was shattered when two German shepherd puppies suddenly jumped from the underbrush playfully yipping and biting at each other. They tumbled into the edge of the water only a few feet from my tripod, and my "perfect scene" looked more like any neighborhood backyard. After a few seconds, the puppies' breathless owner stumbled up. I thought of the park signs which read: "Keep pets on leash," and I glared at the man. To make matters worse, he seemed totally oblivious to the fact that his dogs had disrupted my patient and careful plans to take a photograph. He only watched his dogs play in front of us.

But he wasn't the only one watching.

The "log" which had been near the far bank now had eyes and was moving in our direction. It was moving fast, but without a sound and barely a ripple. It stopped in the middle of some lily pads only a few yards away. Suddenly, the gator sank out of view.

"Sir," I yelled, "there's a gator after your dogs!"

"Where?"

"There!" I pointed to the snout that had surfaced as the gator prepared to make his final lurch for his meal.

The man stared for a few seconds, then he jumped and yelled and chased his puppies away from the shoreline and around the bend of the bayou. They were followed by the V-shaped wake of the hungry gator until the man and his dogs were out of sight.

After the swamp returned to normal, I photographed some of its inhabitants. I was really enjoying the experience, but later that morning, the man returned with his puppies. This time the little ruffians were on leashes. I knew the man's experience with the "floating log" had finally made him realize why the signs were posted, and as the dogs dragged their owner past me in a stumbling trot, I knew why he hadn't bothered with the leashes.

The serenity of the moment was destroyed again. As the man and his dogs lurched by me that morning, I thought about forgetting serious nature photography and taking some shots of the man with his dogs. There's real value in humor photography, you know!

Vegetation provides camouflage for an alligator as he lies in wait for his unsuspecting prey.

White-tailed deer, only a leap away from the refuge of thick cover of the swamplands.

Willows aflame with the emergence of winter.

A wood duck shares a log with two red-eared sliders.

A narcissistic young yellow-crowned watches for a victim.

Juvenile yellow-crowned night heron. Barbara and I enjoyed watching the young birds as they tried to hone their hunting skills. They looked—and in fact were—very awkward as they waded through the swamp scaring their would-be prey.

*Persistence pays off. The
young yellow-crowned night
heron gets a crayfish dinner.*

A skilled hunter, the red-shouldered hawk with a snake in its talons screams defiance to any competitors.

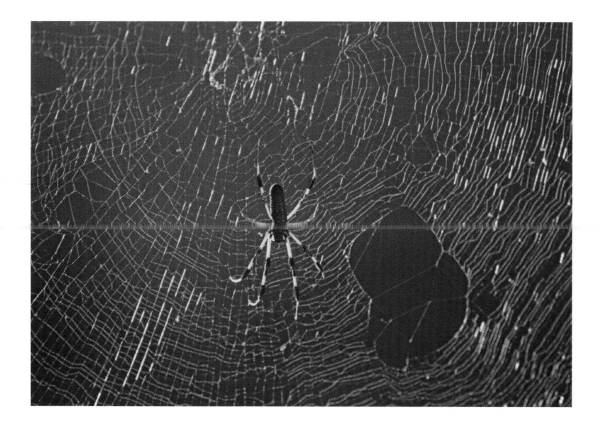

A spider waits patiently on its web, which serves as both home and trap. I have always marveled at spiders' artistic ingenuity and incredible discipline. Whether I'm out in the middle of the woods or in my back yard on a calm morning, the sight of dew glistening on a web fascinates me. I've watched as the wind. . . a dog. . . or a child breaks the guide lines that attach the web to bushes or trees. The spider never rises up and curses the perpetrator. It never pouts in self-pity. It just goes back to work, repairing or replacing the damaged web. And it goes on with life.

Somehow, I think God would be happy if I responded to difficulties the way spiders do.

A drop of water remains on the bill of an adult yellow-crowned night heron after a vain attempt to catch an evening meal.

The barred owl might be more responsible than any other creature for the eerie atmosphere of the swamplands. It is known to some as "the crazy owl" because of its strange looks and noises. The owl's spooky vocalizations can be heard throughout the dark woods day or night.

My friend, Dave, and I placed a caller nearby to make the sounds of a competing male and lure the bird from the woods. We didn't have to wait long. We saw a shadow on the ground, then we heard a soft thud as the owl landed. It peered through the shadows to find its rival. It was ready for a fight! The bird flew from tree to tree while carrying on its crazy monologue.

Fears

Many people fear the swamp. Strange sounds and dark shadows can make us feel uncomfortable. . . and unsafe. We know there are—but we often can't see—hungry alligators and venomous snakes in the murky waters. Each step we take, each paddle stroke we make, warns us to turn back. Our anxiety grows until we can't go any farther.

Like the swamp, the world offers many sinister and hidden things to fear. Evil, pain, and suffering. Rejection, failure, and death. Our fears make us so cautious (and even paranoid) that we resist taking chances. But if we long too much for safety, we isolate ourselves from real life.

Paul wrote in his letter to the Philippians, "Do not be anxious about anything, but in everything, by prayer and petition, with thanksgiving, present your requests to God. And the peace of God which transcends all understanding, will guard your hearts and minds in Christ Jesus" (Philippians 4:6-7).

"But how," some of us ask, "can I trust God when I see so many bad things happening to people?"

Paul anticipated that question in verses 4 and 5: "Rejoice in the Lord always. I will say it again: Rejoice! Let your gentleness be evident to all. The Lord is near."

The Lord is near. We aren't alone as we walk through life's swamplands. God is with us—"as close as our breath"—and he guides us as we face difficulties. Paul knew what he was talking about. He had been ridiculed, shipwrecked, stoned, whipped, and thrown in prison. He was rejected by his friends. He had looked death in the face many times. But he also knew Jesus had prayed in the garden to the Father, "My prayer is not that you take them out of the world, but that you protect them from the evil one" (John 17:15). This prayer was uttered two thousand years ago for all who believe in Jesus as Lord and Savior. . . for you and me.

Our lives, like the swamps, are filled with wonder, beauty, and challenges. If we learn to see through the shadows, we will realize we can live with confidence because God is near.

*Predators and prey alike
find shelter in the woods.*

A barred owl.

*A white-tailed doe in a
hardwood river bottom.*

So do not fear, for I am with you;
  do not be dismayed, for I am your God.
I will strengthen you and help you;
  I will uphold you with my righteous right
hand.

Isaiah 41:10

Desert

The wild animals honor me,
the jackals and the owls,
because I provide water in the desert
and streams in the wasteland,
to give drink to my people, my chosen.
Isaiah 43:20

If you could pick one word to describe the desert, what would it be? Dry, hot, hostile, barren, vast, inhospitable? All of these fit, but none of them describes the desert entirely. The desert is all these things, but it is more—much more. If I could personify the desert, I would say it is patient. The barren landscape sits apparently lifeless day after day until moisture finally comes to quench its thirst and transform it into a sudden, brief, magnificent spectacle of vibrant colors. It's worth the wait!

A rare thunder storm
quenches the desert's thirst.

The Source of Life

Appearing like waves in an ocean, mountains crest above a sea of sand which seems to stretch on forever. The surface of the desert is rough, desolate, and inhospitable, but in spite of this harsh climate, life thrives there. And *because* of the harsh climate, some very unusual animals exist in the desert by conserving their resources and by using unique methods of finding food and water. Some animals common to other parts of the country have adapted to desert life. Mountain lions have adapted so well that they now survive almost exclusively in the most remote and rugged regions of the West, protected by the vast expanse of desert. Golden eagles soar above these mountains where they, like the black bear, have found refuge from the burgeoning pressures of human population which threaten their existence.

Far below the mountain peaks are creatures which can survive the searing heat of the desert floor. Jack rabbits have long ears for ventilation—and long legs for speed, a necessary ingredient for survival because that most efficient predator, the coyote, is constantly on the prowl for a rabbit dinner. Coyotes usually hunt in groups to cover more of the vast terrain and utilize less energy. During the scorching daylight hours, mule deer, javelina, fox, roadrunners, quail, snakes, and lizards take shelter in the shadows of rocks and plants.

When the sun dips below the horizon and the temperature drops, the desert springs to life. The never-ending search for food and water—and the never-ending struggle to avoid *being* food—begins again each dusk.

Without water in the form of rain, dew, fog, or springs, the desert would be truly barren, but this lifesource is hard to find. Animals and plants have ingenious ways to locate and preserve this precious liquid. Cactus, trees, grasses, and other plants send roots through the sandy soil to find any hint of moisture. And animals must eat water-rich plants to survive, or get enough liquid from prey they devour. Birds and insects find moisture in the flowers, bugs, and seeds they eat.

During the rare periods of steady rain, dry creek beds become torrents of water. Low spots become pools, and here, every slimy, feathered, scaly, and furry critter gathers to drink. Desert plants explode in colorful blossoms, and the insects buzz as they make the most of the opportunity. But soon, the blazing sun parches these oases into dust again, and the struggle for survival takes on its normal rhythms.

The Chihuahuan Desert spreads over 140,000 square miles of north-

The coyote is a survivor, able to adapt to the most barren environments as well as to the areas where civilization has spread.

ern Mexico and the southwest United States. Through the middle of this dry, desolate land runs a ribbon of life: the Rio Grande. The "Big River" belies its name as it meanders its slow and shallow course as a sliver of murky liquid. From its headwaters in the rocky eastern slopes of the San Juan Mountains, it gradually winds its way toward the Mexican border. The pressures of agriculture and industry sap its strength as it passes through "The Valley" of South Texas, and by the time it reaches the Gulf, the Rio Grande is only a shadow of a truly great river. Back in the desert, people are attracted to this river because of the relatively untouched landscape. The beauty of barrenness.

Barbara and I were on our way to Lahitas, a town on the Rio Grande, for dinner at the Starlight Cafe, which on this night offered poetry readings by some of the locals. As we passed through the ghost town of Terlingua, Barbara asked me to stop at the town's cemetery. The setting sun bathed the land in warm shades. As I stopped the truck on the dusty road, Barbara grabbed the camera and scrambled out the door to capture the scene on film. She walked toward the western edge of the burial ground. Behind her, I noticed a large canvas on an easel in the midst of the tilted, neglected crosses on the graves. The man sitting in front of it divided his attention between the canvas and the setting sun. His hand moved in broad brush strokes. I was intrigued, and I wanted to meet him. Barbara got there first, and as I approached, she introduced me to her new friend, Miguel. He explained that he had traveled from Spain to paint images of the desert Southwest. In fluent English, he told us about his travels over many miles to complete his project which had been commissioned by a wealthy benefactor in New York. This spot, he believed, embodied the characteristics and the beauty of the region. Miguel had done his homework on the old cemetery, and he explained that most of those buried there were Mexicans who had come to work in the mine shafts in the hills nearby. They wanted to earn higher wages in the United States, but some had paid with their lives when the tunnels collapsed on them. The headstones told us they had come—and died—as early as the beginning of the century.

Miguel showed us his camper, which was now his home. He also let us see some of his finished work. Barbara wanted to buy one of the pieces, but it was a part of the commissioned work. He instead offered us some of his paintings which had not been spoken for. We asked the price, and he gave us a figure that was more than the price of our new pickup! Thanks anyway, Miguel. We settled for a photograph of him in front of his work. As the last moments of light passed, we said good-bye to Miguel and drove on to the Starlight Cafe.

Barbara and I enjoyed our dinner in the dimly lit cafe. We listened to poets as they took turns at the microphone in the middle of the part-time

Blooms of the prickly pear cactus burst open after a rain.

dance floor. Suddenly, I heard my name spoken behind me. I turned to see a man with long hair and a beard who had the advantage of knowing me though I didn't recognize him. After he introduced himself, I was amazed to learn that I had known him six years earlier. I asked the perfunctory question, "What have you been doing the last few years?" He explained—without divulging details—that he had been in some trouble with the IRS. The desert was his sanctuary from life's pressures. He left our table after a few minutes and sat at the microphone to recite his poem about tracks being left in the soft banks of a river. The impressions animals left in the mud marked their passing. His poem seemed to be a metaphor of his own experience. Like the coyote and the mountain lion in his poem, this man had come to the river in the desert to find refuge and nourishment.

Rains came too late for this juniper, whose shadow creeps across the desert in front of the Guadalupe Mountains.

Some people come to the desert for solitude and peace; they are attracted by the stark beauty. Many come to find riches. Like the mine workers from a century ago, Mexican nationals cross the Rio Grande today in search of prosperity. Many are captured before they get far, but thousands more make their way through the desert each year in the hope of finding jobs. Many endure tremendous hardships on their journey. Some find prosperity, but too many find only greater pressures and heartaches than those they left behind. The price may be high for many who come, but hope fuels their desperate search and their willingness to take these risks.

The desert is a unique environment, but one aspect of it is common in every setting, for people in the richest countries and the poorest, on Wall Street and on the dirt road in Ethiopia. The heart of every man and woman on earth searches for meaning. Some search for wealth, others for fame or beauty, and still others for love and acceptance. Like the pool of water in the desert, these things will pass away. Jesus spoke of water, a new kind of water which truly satisfies our thirst. He told the Samaritan woman as she drew water from a well:

> *Whoever drinks of this water will thirst again, but*
> *whoever drinks of the water that I shall give him will never*
> *thirst. But the water that I shall give him will become in him*
> *a fountain of water springing up into everlasting life.*
> *John 4:13-14*

Jesus knew temptation, rejection, and heartache—more than any person ever has. He knew what thirst felt like, and he quenched that thirst with the love and strength of his Father. He offers us living water to quench our deepest thirst for meaning, for wholeness, for forgiveness, and for intimacy with him. If we accept and drink deeply of him, our lives will be forever transformed.

Ground squirrel.

Mule deer travel a ridge through the desert.

The acorn woodpecker
thrives in the mountainous
regions of the Chihuahuan
Desert. These birds store
acorns in holes they have
hammered from trees.

Opposite: Chisos Mountains,
Big Bend National Park.

A roadrunner near the Rio Grande River. These birds are prolific killers of all kinds of reptiles, including rattlesnakes.

A javelina blocks a desert trail. These peculiar animals have poor eyesight, they are noisy, and they smell awful! They also have razor-sharp teeth! Barbara and I were hiking in Big Bend National Park when we came across a herd of these pigs. We let this one have the trail for as long as he wanted it. (We didn't want to experience those tusks "up close and personal"!)

Reflection

I stopped for lunch at the only restaurant in Dell City. A man in a cowboy hat invited me to join him, so I pulled a chair up to his table. As I ate my enchiladas, he told me his story. He moved to Texas from Illinois years before to pursue his two greatest passions: ranching and ministry. He spread the word of God through a series of missions he helped build south of the border a few miles away. He asked about my faith, and I told him I'm a Christian. He asked what I was doing in the area. I explained I was photographing the mountains nearby. His eyes lit up. He leaned forward, and he told me about a place where the reflection of the Guadalupe Mountains could be seen in the salt lake to the west as the sun sank low. After our visit, I hurried out of the restaurant to be there at the right moment for this image.

A reflection is but an imitation of the original. Any ripple can cause a distortion of the image. We are exhorted by Paul: "Be imitators of God, therefore, as dearly loved children and live a life of love, just as Christ loved us and gave himself up for us as a fragrant offering and sacrifice to God" (Ephesians 5:1-2).

Our imperfections make this an impossible task. We could never love as perfectly or sacrifice as wholly as Jesus did, but we can begin to remove the hate or jealousy or any other stones we toss into the water of our lives. By God's grace, we can calm the ripples.

I live in a wasteland
Of hopes grown old—
O Who is the God
Of the barren of soul?

The desert wind whispers
Through parched lips so thin,
"No landscape,
No wanderer
Is forgotten of Him."
    Jennie Takemoto

Even the dry sands of the desert can provide nourishment for creatures like these butterflies swarming the blooms of desert plants.

The red-tailed hawk's keen eyesight allows him to find prey at great distances across the desert floor.

My friend, Steve, invited me to see the land he patrols as a game warden in the Chihuahuan Desert where it reaches into West Texas. We drove for hours each day along the desert roads talking about God's awesome creation and our role in it. One morning we drove east as clouds hung low over the desert. After a while, the road took us up into the clouds as a light snow began to fall. These roads were some of the the roughest I had ever travelled. When we reached our destination, we stepped out of the truck into temperatures that were at least 20 degrees colder than those we had left in the lower desert. The snows fell harder and harder. In this winter wonderland, we saw mule deer, javelina, and desert bighorn sheep. It was a rare day for me—and a rare day for the desert as well.

Late in the afternoon, we descended from the Sierra Diablo Mountains and headed west toward town. The sky, which had been gray and heavy all day, parted at the horizon. As the sun dipped below the mountains, it set the clouds on fire.

Opposite: Desert bighorns.

*Terlingua cemetery. One of
my favorite images is this
one Barbara captured, a
scene of desolation and
hope in the desert of West
Texas.*

So we fix our eyes not on what is seen, but on what is unseen. For what is seen is temporary, but what is unseen is eternal.

II Corinthians 4:18

Hills Near Home

Because God created the natural—
invented it out of his love and artistry—
it demands our reverence.
    C.S. Lewis, *God in the Dock*

I grew up on the edge of the Texas Hill Country, where I learned to hunt and fish. When school and work took me away, I often thought of these hills. I longed for the clear waters of rocky streams where I could see bass in the still, deep pools. I missed the white-tailed deer that foraged for acorns under oaks on gently rolling hills.

I missed the place of my childhood, and I took every chance to return there. But when I went back, things weren't exactly as I had remembered. Maybe they never are. More subdivisions. . . more signs along the highways . . . fewer uninterrupted views of hills and sky.

But the hills are still beautiful. They'll always be my earthly home, full of old memories, and now making new ones with Barbara and our twins, Micah and Anna.

It was the first cold morning of Fall, and the drop in temperature made steam rise off the water and fill the Pedernales River valley.

Fishing the Pedernales

A few years ago, Barbara gave me a fly rod for Christmas. I could hardly wait to try it out, so I made plans to go to the Pedernales River (pronounced, as all Texans know, "Perdenales") to wet a hook. I set up shop at the water's edge and began sawing the air in my first attempts to keep the fly airborne.

I hooked a tree.

I hooked my ear.

After a while, a great blue heron flew in from down-river. He landed, took a second to gather himself, then turned to glare at me. Maybe he had seen me at a distance and he wanted a good laugh. Maybe he realized I wasn't going to be much competition for him as he fished from that particular pool that day. I'm not sure of the reason for his sudden appearance, but I quickly realized that this bird was acting strange. He hopped from rock to rock until he came quite near me. I put down the rod and reached into my backpack to pull out a camera with a 50mm lens. (I brought that camera to record the day's catch. Oh, well. . . .)

The morning sun peeked over the surrounding hills to bathe the scene in warm light as the heron fished a few yards away. The breeding season had him in a fog. Maybe he thought I was a rival—or worse, a lady heron! He soon recognized his mistake, and he coiled for a take off. I took this shot just before his wariness got the best of him.

He took flight, headed up the river on slow, steady wingbeats, and vanished around the next bend. If his head cleared, there was still time for him to get in a good day's fishing. I'm sure he had better luck than I had that day!

Sunrise over the Pedernales River Valley.

Opposite: The great blue heron is normally a wary bird. Other animals watch this heron, which has the advantage of an extremely long neck so it can see a long way, to make sure all is safe.

The scrub jay is a raucous bird found throughout the Texas Hill Country.

Maple leaves turn brilliant colors in early fall.

Let the fields be jubilant, and everything in them.
Then all the trees of the forest will sing for joy.
Psalm 96:12

Cypress trees form an arch over a Hill Country creek.

Opposite: A white-tailed doe bounds for the safety of the hills.

A cardinal with fluffed
feathers finds shelter from
the cold in a thicket.

*Wood ducks flush from
a creek.*

Spring is the time of plenty in the natural world. Winter's chill has departed, and the scorching days of summer are still in the distance. Life abounds as dragonflies and flowers awake from their slumber, and birds of all kinds resume their courtship. The bobwhite quail sings his namesake song in hope of attracting a mate. I answered this quail's call, and to my surprise, he approached close enough to my truck for me to take his portrait.

A tender moment between
white-tailed fawns.

A butterfly drinks the nectar of a flower.

Fawns are usually born in the spring so their nursing mothers can take advantage of the abundance of food. If undisturbed, a fawn will stay hidden in the tall grass where its mother has left it until she returns.

Why, intrigued ignorance asked, did wild
   things so often choose to stool on rocks,
   stumps, and other elevations?
Common sense replied: Maybe for the view.
   John Graves, *Goodbye to a River*

The raccoon is a most
interesting animal. It has
the strange habits of wash-
ing its food before it eats. .
. and leaving its poop on
any object it chooses.

A stream, bordered by sycamore trees in fall foliage, winds through the hills.

The Hummingbird
and the Deer

Two inhabitants of the hill country near our home, the black-chinned hummingbird and the white-tailed deer, offer a constant reminder of the amazing details in God's creation. We enjoyed watching the hummingbirds feed on "native plants" in our yard, and we were entertained by their culinary acrobatics and their mid-air battles during the breeding season. A hummingbird is a tiny animal (the smallest is the Cuban "bee hummingbird," barely two-and-a-quarter inches long), but the message it tells about its Creator is as powerful and clear as the ones sent by an elephant or a whale. Each animal has its unique place in nature. Each one possesses beauty and majesty. And each is perfectly crafted by the loving and sometimes humorous—hand of God. A hummingbird's wings beat up to 78 times a second. It can hover, fly backward, forward, and even upside down! It uses all these techniques when it fights for territory. The only time these tiny warriors stop fighting is when they refuel on the nectar of the flowers. . . and that's just so they can regain their strength to fight again!

We saw these three bucks quite often during the summer as they browsed on plants and drank from the stream. They needed sustenance to nourish their new antlers growing under velvet covering. The antlers of bucks are shed every spring and regrown every summer and fall. In fact, antlers are the fastest-growing things in the animal kingdom. These boney structures grow up to a half inch in a day if they are supplied with nutrient-rich blood by the velvet, which also protects the antlers' sensitive surface. In the fall, the antlers are at their full measure and glory. The bucks rake the velvet off by scraping and polishing their antlers on tree trunks, branches, and fence posts.

Over the years, I've learned to look for evidences of this process in every season of the year. In the spring, I find the discarded antlers from the year before; in the summer, I see the deer with antlers growing and developing; and in the fall, I can see the proud bucks showing off their year's growth. And if I look closely, I can also find scrapes and rub marks on hundreds of trees and posts. These are silent messages that growth in the animal kingdom—like any growth in my life—often comes through a mysterious combination of nourishment and struggle.

Scrapes and rub marks show up on people's lives —including mine. In one of the most encouraging passages in the Scriptures, Paul tells us God has a purpose for our struggles: "We rejoice in our sufferings, because we know that suffering produces perseverance; perseverance, character; and character, hope. And hope does not disappoint us, because God has poured out his love into our hearts by the Holy Spirit, whom he has given to us" (Romans 5:3-5). In our difficulties, we are nourished by the love of God, and we have hope that he will somehow bring good out of absolutely anything we face. As we realize the goodness and wisdom of our loving Father, we have reason to rejoice.

Maple and cherry trees along the Sabinal River. Barbara decided to sleep in on this drizzly November morning, so her father, Oscar, volunteered to keep me company on the early morning drive from their home in Kerrville to Lost Maples State Natural Area, which is at the headwaters of the Sabinal. We arrived early, before the crowd. We enjoyed the peace and quiet of the park. To me, the most wonderful thing was the array of colors along the river, but Oscar is colorblind, and I could never—no matter how hard I tried—explain in words the incredible splashes of color scattered on the hills that morning.

That time with Oscar made me thankful for the ability to see things I usually take for granted. . . and it also gave me a new appreciation for Oscar, who graciously took me to observe and enjoy things he knew he couldn't see.

Opposite: Black-capped chickadee.

"Pictures of Weeds?"

As the saying goes, "It was a hundred degrees in the shade!" But it was even hotter than that in my pickup that afternoon. I parked at the edge of an old corral whose rotting fence matched the condition of the barn. Years ago, this structure had provided shelter and feed for livestock on the ranch, but now, only thistles grew in the tired earth inside the old corral.

I sat in that blast furnace, which doubled as a truck, sweating every drop of water I had drunk from the gallon jug laying empty on the seat next to me. The telephoto lens rested on the half-rolled down window. Soon, a cloud of dust from down the road told me I had company. The pickup pulled up next to me, and Barbara's grandfather rolled down his window. (Not too far. He didn't want too much of the air conditioning to escape!)

Years before, Pappy had worked cattle in this pen to provide for the family. We talked for a few minutes, then Pappy asked with a smile, "You taking pictures of those weeds?"

I laughed and nodded. I knew good and well what he was thinking. Without another word, Pappy's window climbed up, and the pickup headed back up the road, trailing a cloud of dust.

I turned my attention back to the thistles, and I watched finches, hummingbirds, bees, and butterflies dine on their favorite parts of the weeds. The creatures flew around the old corral, the camera shutter blinked, and the sweat rolled off every part of my body. Thankfully, God knows more than just what's on the surface of our lives. He looks past the weeds to see what we can be.

Suddenly the air was filled with a strange sound. It came from the hill beyond the weeds. A red-tailed hawk soared over the hill screaming its warning to another hawk which was trying to steal its talon-grabbed squirrel!

The shutter blinked again.

*Waterfall on a spring-fed
creek.*

As the deer pants for streams of water,
so my soul pants for you, O God.
Psalm 42:1

Plains

If you stand on the plains, it seems like you can see the end of the world. You feel so small and alone. The wail of a coyote carries over miles of grasslands, canyons, and dry riverbeds to reach your ears to let you know there is another presence somewhere on this endless sea of land. Your searching eyes find a herd of antelope on the horizon far away and a dark speck floating on the winds above the plains. These creatures remind you of a Maker who watches and guides you.

Antelope graze as darkness approaches.

The Great Horned Owl

I saw one silhouetted at dawn on the tallest mesquite tree. Occasionally I saw one on a telephone pole overlooking their hunting grounds as the sun dipped below the horizon. Rarely—very rarely—I saw a great horned owl in the broad daylight.

Though I seldom saw them, I knew these silent-winged hunters were out there because I saw the signs: a pile of fur and some dried blood told of a successful hunt the night before; a neighbor's cat was missing from the ranks at the breakfast roll call. They were out there, all right.

I had hoped to photograph one of these magnificent birds on our family ranch, but I had a problem. The human eye and the camera's lens don't see too well in the dark when owls are active. The one in this picture chose a big mesquite tree for a roost and had a shadowy snooze during the bright, hot hours of the day. As I drove the pickup down the dirt road under the tree's outstretched branches, I didn't see the bird until I had startled him. It flew across an open field and landed in another mesquite about 300 yards from the road.

I drove up to the ranch house, and from the kitchen window, I peered at the bird through binoculars. I could barely make out the dark shape nestled into the shadows of the treeline. My mom fixed breakfast and coffee as my father and I devised a strategy to capture the owl on film.

Dad dropped me off at the mouth of the draw that ran from the county road south along the line of trees where the owl was perched. I'm sure my dad wondered how I could expect to walk on noisy, crunching dead twigs and dried grass to sneak up on a creature that can hear a mouse scurrying 50 yards away!

The yellow eyes of the owl were trained on me as soon as I could see him—about 100 yards away. Since my stealth was, shall we say, ineffective, I left the cover of the draw and began crawling straight toward him, pushing the heavy camera equipment all the way.

The owl just watched.

Several ranchers passed by on the road. They slowed down and stared at the strange sight of a man crawling with heavy boxes through a field in the morning sun!

The owl only watched.

Grass burrs impaled my hands and knees. My mind was filled with vivid thoughts of rattlesnakes in the high grass. I struggled on.

The owl still watched.

Finally, I was close enough. I finished the roll of film in my camera, then I reached in my pocket for another roll. Empty! After all I'd gone through to get so close to this owl, I kicked myself for forgetting to bring more film.

I sat and watched, entranced by the piercing yellow eyes. The owl then left its perch. With a few strokes on silent wings, it—like my disappointment—was gone, leaving me with a vivid memory of this mysterious bird.

The great horned owl was created to hunt at night. Large eyes allow them to see in almost total darkness. Facial disks enhance the sound-gathering abilities of their ears, and the soft edges of their feathers allow them to fly silently.

The setting sun brings
darkness over the land.

Opposite: The last of the
sun's rays catches a great
horned owl as it begins its
hunt.

A kestrel stretches a wing in preparation for flight. Also known as a "sparrow hawk," the kestrel is the smallest falcon in North America.

Opposite: Mule deer buck. These deer get their name from their mule-like ears.

Mallard ducks take flight
on angelic wings.

Mourning dove.

Praise him, sun. . .

. . . and moon, praise him, all you shining stars.

Psalm 148:3

Sandhill cranes cross the moon on their descent to a lake at Muleshoe National Wildlife Refuge. I had been taking pictures for several hours as the cranes returned from the grain fields nearby, and finally a flight passed in front of the moon. I took several exposures with the 600mm lens, and I decided to try a different angle with the 300mm lens. As I crouched down, I accidentally kicked the legs of the tripod holding the larger lens. Thirty pounds of camera equipment struck me on the on the head and knocked me to the ground! When the camera and lens hit, the film door flew open, exposing all the film inside. I recovered in time to get one more picture before the cranes touched down. I was left with a gash on my head. . . and the image I had hoped for.

Prairie dogs stay alert for danger.

A burrowing owl finds a vantage point over the flat land. Prairie dogs and burrowing owls live in the same network of chambers and tunnels that make up underground housing on the plains. These ecosystems are called "prairie dog towns."

Vision

Antelope can see movement at four miles and can run in excess of fifty miles an hour. These incredible abilities make the antelope elusive prey to their main enemy, the coyote, but antelope don't always run from their nemesis. They have been known to chase coyotes which attack their young.

We could take our cue from the antelope. God has given us the vision and discernment to recognize danger in our lives, and he has given us the strength to flee. But running isn't always the answer. Sometimes we have to stand and fight for what is true, and sometimes we need to look beyond ourselves and rescue those in need.

Paul instructed us to run from some things: "Flee the evil desires of youth, and pursue righteousness, faith, love and peace" (II Timothy 2:22). But he also encouraged us to know when to stand and fight: "Put on the full armor of God so that you can take your stand against the devil's schemes" (Ephesians 6:11).

. . . the rim of the sunrise that shoots time dead with golden arrows and puts to flight all phantasmal shapes.
C. S. Lewis, *The Great Divorce*

A pair of red-tailed hawks await the day from the branches of a mesquite tree.

A meadowlark grips the stalks of withered sunflowers.

The Homecoming

Like my grandfather, Joe Matthews, my mother and her sister were born in the shadow of Double Mountain on the rolling plains of Texas. At times this land is harsh, but at other moments, it holds a beauty unique to these red dirt plains. The day it wore its finest garments was the day of my grandfather's homecoming.

My memories of my grandfather are plentiful and vivid. As though it were yesterday, I recall being a young boy sitting on the floor of the living room where he and grandmother Erna lived. As I eagerly listened, he told stories of his younger days when he was a child and when he was a cowboy. He talked about his hunting trips, animals he had loved or feared, and assorted folklore of the plains. I was fascinated by him and his tales.

The first story I remember was actually a prank he pulled on my sister, Tanya, and me when we were little kids. He said there were people who were buried in Double Mountain cemetery a long, long time ago, and their ghosts would answer you from their graves. If you holler to them, "What are you doing down there?" they'll reply, "Nothing!" Tanya and I leaned back and looked at each other with wide, wondering eyes. One of us figured out pretty quickly that he was pulling our legs and said, "Granddad, that isn't true! They can't talk!" But he assured us that it was true and we could hear them for ourselves. A few minutes later, Tanya and I jumped into his Jeep along with Erna, Mom, and Dad. We drove over to the cemetery a half mile north of their house. Granddad pulled through the gates and parked the Jeep. He pointed to the northeast corner of the small graveyard and said, "Go over there and holler at those folks. You'll see I was telling the truth."

Tanya and I cautiously walked down to the grave site he had pointed out. I leaned toward the ground and whispered, "Wh-wh-what are you doing down there?" We listened. No response.

We stepped a little closer, and I tried again, "Wh-wh-wh-what are you doing down there?" Tanya and I strained our ears for the answer, but we heard only silence.

We turned and ran back to the safety of our elders and told Joe that the ghosts didn't say anything. He looked down and shook his head. We thought he was commiserating with us. Later we realized that he had been laughing on the inside, waiting for us to understand that the "ghosts" had said exactly what he said they would say: Nothing! Joe enjoyed recounting that incident about Tanya and me for many years.

Tanya and I weren't the only ones who were the focus of his schemes. Joe

played sports in the tiny town of Peacock, Texas, which is located twelve miles from the family's ranch. One of his favorite tales of his youth was about the time he and his teammates were showering after a school basketball game. Somebody spotted a "plumber's helper" (a plunger) in the corner of the shower and decided to see what it would do on exposed, wet skin. This unnamed character picked up the plunger and smashed it on the back of an unsuspecting friend! The plunger got stuck! It took half the team to pull the handle and the other half to hold the victim (who was making things more difficult by shouting and writhing in pain!). Finally, the suction broke, and the boy was freed. . . with a huge, red, temporary tattoo on his backside! Joe never said who did the dastardly deed, but we had a good idea who the perpetrator was! He told us the victim was a boy named "Clabber" Reese. We had a good laugh about that nickname, and that led us to another story about some people in Stonewall County.

Downtown: Peacock, Texas.

Joe's family included his sister, Aunt "Pig" (I can't guess how such a pretty woman got a handle like that!), "Toad," "Buck," and their cousin who married "Sheep." Joe's acquaintances included "Wham," "Wad" (a woman), and "Toot'n." (I can make an educated guess about this one!) Nicknames like these are common in that area even today. Recently, my Mom asked a lady at the church about the man who lived across the street. The lady glanced at the house and with a quizzical look said, "You know, I have never known his real name. Everybody just calls him 'Son-in-law.'" Such is life in rural America!

A tornado hit this farming community in 1914 and took much of the town of Peacock with it. The twister destroyed the dry goods store and scattered merchandise over the county. The store had just received a big order of women's shoes. Joe recalled, "After the cyclone, times were so hard that even the boys around town were seen wearing women's shoes for several years!"

Joe lived through some very lean years on the plains, and he knew the value of a dollar. . . especially if he didn't have one. His views on hunting were influenced by this lack of resources. Joe was astounded by the price of ammunition. He used to say that the only good way to hunt quail was to find their tracks on a cold, snowy day, and then follow them to the place where they were hiding from the cold, north wind—most likely on the south side of a bush, tree, or cactus. When you found them huddled together, you could "kill six or eight with one shot." This economical and practical perspective made Joe a bit skeptical about "the city boy" who came to the ranch house each year asking if Joe would take him to hunt quail.

Joe's skepticism didn't prevent him from being amused by people who weren't at home in the country. He sometimes let them hunt on his property, but he'd get a good laugh out of the bargain. Joe's favorite tale about city folks was about a bunch who came to the ranch and offered him the chance to hunt behind a highly trained and skilled bird dog. Acting as if they were doing him a big favor, Joe said "yes" and ducked inside the house to get his shotgun and shells. When he came out the door, he noticed the raised eyebrows and barely muffled snickers of the

men as they got a glimpse of Joe's beat-up, single-shot .410. Joe told the men, "Follow me," and he jumped in his Jeep. The men followed in their spit-shined, fancy, air-conditioned truck with a trailer and dog kennel on the back. Joe took them to the grainfields where he knew the coveys were hiding that day. He parked the Jeep and climbed out. The men unsheathed their polished guns from their cases, then they slid dozens of shotgun shells into bird bags around their waists. With the air of a royal ceremony, one of the men introduced Joe to his prized dog, Toddy. He opened the kennel and freed the sleek, wiry pointer. The dog, in a splendid display of field trial obedience, leaped from the trailer, hit the ground on the run and disappeared over the first terrace in the field! The man yelled, "Toddy! Heel, Toddy! Heel, boy!" But the dog was long gone!

Without a word, Joe climbed into his old Jeep and headed back home.

Joe later heard that Toddy was finally found about a week later several miles away. Joe said there was no need for a dog for hunting quail— especially a "city dog" named after a fancy drink!

"City boy" wasn't an endearing term to Joe. At times he used it to refer to my Dad who had replaced him as the man in his daughter's life. Dad grew up in the city and could be a "wise acre" on occasion (actually, on many occasions!). Joe was determined to teach his son-in-law a few lessons about hunting. One of these lessons was about "the city boy" and the badger. Dad and Joe were hunting in the pasture one day, and they came across a badger. The animal turned and ran, but he tried to crawl into a hole made by a smaller animal. He got stuck! Joe convinced my Dad to tie a rope around the badger's back legs, toss the rope over a tree limb, and yank the critter out. When Dad yanked the rope, the badger came out. . . and came unglued! It was like roping a tornado—with claws and teeth! After a little while, Joe figured Dad had learned his lesson. He then, shall we say, disposed of the situation.

The ranch house where we listened to Joe's stories was built on a pier and beam foundation with ample crawl space underneath. During the winter, rattlesnakes used this area under the floor as a den. Sometimes we could hear them buzzing as we walked over them. Another good snake den was an old cistern about 50 yards from the house. A cistern (for you "city folks" who don't know) is a hole in the ground lined with concrete. A well collects underground water; a cistern collects rain water. Many years ago this particular cistern gave Joe's family and any passers-by a cool drink of reddish water. But for the past few years, it had collected only trash and rattlesnakes. One day my Dad saw about a dozen rattlers sunning themselves on the trash heap inside the cistern. He went to the house and found some gasoline and matches. He returned to the cistern, doused the snakes, lit a match, and tossed it in. . . nothing. The match had gone out before it reached the soaked—and furious—snakes. He tried again. Same result. Then he decided to go back to the house and get some paper so the flame would burn a little longer. By the time he got back to the cistern, the fumes had built up

Badgers may be the toughest and most ornery of all Texans. When they are disturbed, they growl, hiss, bare their teeth, and puff out their bodies for a more menacing appearance. As is the case with most badgers which aren't actually threatened, this one's bark was much worse than its bite. It bluffed a charge before heading for home. It reappeared for one more look at me, the intruder.

inside the hole, and when Dad dropped the burning paper in there. . .
BOOOOMMMMM!!!!

Joe had been watching from a distance. He related his observation: "Ol' city boy went flying backwards several feet in the air and landed on his back. Trash and dead snakes rained down on him! It was quite a sight!"

No one was safe from being embarrassed by Joe's schemes. . . except for Erna. Joe met her when he was finishing high school in Peacock. She had gone to Peacock to teach, and when Joe laid eyes on her, he thought she was "the prettiest thing I'd ever seen!" They married during the summer after Joe finished high school. Many people (including Joe) wondered why a proper lady like Erna would fall for a rambunctious cowboy, but it was a match made in heaven. Joe could not have found a woman who would support him more entirely or love him more unconditionally than Erna, nor could Erna have been blessed with someone who would cherish her more than Joe obviously did.

Daybreak at the Matthews' ranch.

After they married, they left the ranch. They decided that scratching out a living on the red dirt plains was an impossible task. Years later when they retired, they moved back to the ranch. Joe hired a carpenter to build a special room on the existing ranch house. He demanded the room be built air-tight so the red dirt that blew on the howling winds couldn't get in and soil Erna's yellow velvet, Victorian furniture or the organ she loved to play. Erna told us many times how sweet it was for Joe to build her that room so that she could serenade the coyotes roaming the plains outside her window.

Joe never belittled or embarrassed Erna, but he couldn't pass up the chance to tell a good story about her lifelong battle with the automobile. Erna couldn't judge long distances very well, and she had a hard time keeping dents out of the bumper and fenders of every vehicle she drove. Joe was patient with her. He was determined that she become an adequate, if not good, driver. He said she was really improving—until the day they set out to build a fence. Erna was to drive the Model A truck slowly through the pasture as Joe threw out fence posts at certain intervals. Everything was going fine until she drove under a low limb of a mesquite tree. She looked around to make sure Joe was all right, but he had ducked down to avoid the limb, and she couldn't see him. At that exact moment, she ran over an old fence post that bounced the truck off the ground. Erna thought the bump was Joe! He reappeared in a few seconds from the bed of the pickup, but his resurrection did little to calm her fears. The incident scared her so badly that she vowed never to drive again. . . ever. It was 40 years later, when they returned to the ranch, that Joe convinced Erna to try again. Each time we arrived for a visit, Joe, with a twinkle in his eye, showed us fresh dents and scrapes on the car, the gates, and the trees. Yes, Erna was indeed driving again!

Joe knew that the art of telling a good tale involved creative license. Most of his stories had fallen on the same ears many times over the years, but we always looked forward to the parts of the "yarns" that grew with time. He was a proud father and grandfather. He loved to tell people of my exploits on the football field,

and I'm sure some of the details grew to legendary proportions! (I hope so, anyway!)

Joe taught tough lessons, and he was a tough man. Both were the results of the times and the place where he lived. I was with him when he nearly lost his thumb while he was working cows in a loading chute, and I was at his side another time when he broke four ribs falling from the roof of the house when he was replacing shingles. Typically, he barely even grimaced no matter how bad the pain might be. . . until he was in Erna's comforting, loving, caring presence.

Though he was tough and mischievous, Joe was also very tender and loving. He sat with his sister in her small room at the nursing home for hours on end. She didn't recognize him, but he loved her and he wanted to be there for her. He never met a stranger, and he would drive miles out of his way to listen to a friend who had a problem. The years softened the rough edges of this strong man, and he even learned to love people from the cities. He and Erna moved to a retirement center, and Joe met, consoled, loved, and laughed with every person who lived there. He joined a choir and sang about his Lord and Savior, Jesus Christ, who had been the source of his tenderness and strength.

I remember special times with this very special man. The man I saw in the late summer of 1993 was physically changed. He was very sick, barely clinging to life. Joe was tired and weakened from fighting the cancer that had formed in his lungs months before, and which had now spread throughout his body. He was no longer larger than life. He was thin and frail. Joe's appearance shocked me, but as I spent time with him, I realized he was the same wonderful man. His body was weak, but his heart was still just as strong, despite the pain the disease had brought him and the rest of his family. His wonderful sense of humor was still there. He still cherished Erna. And he still trusted God. Before I left his room that day, I saw that same proud sparkle in his eyes.

I knew it was my last time to enjoy being with him.

Rains came to the rolling plains in the fall of 1993. Those rains brought new life to the fields and animals. Wildflowers seemed to explode from the ground! The land between the Double Mountain Fork and Salt Fork of the Brazos River had never looked more splendid. Joe Matthews' body was buried amid the tears of many who loved him, but his soul was already home.

I go to the cemetery on the hill now and again when I visit those red dirt plains. The cemetery speaks to me now, not in the prank of a ghost's voice, but in the memories of a man who enjoyed and shared life and love and his Savior with me.

Sunflower field on the plains.

Opposite: Double Mountain Cemetery.

Double Mountain under a sky painted by our Creator with clouds and a setting sun.

Come to me, all you who are weary and
burdened, and I will give you rest.
Matthew 11:28

Mountain Meadows and River Valleys

In the last days the mountain of the Lord's
temple will be established as chief among
the mountains;
it will be raised above the hills, and all nations
will stream to it.
Isaiah 2:2

Mountain scenes always inspire us. Majestic, snow-covered crags reach the clouds. They speak of God's greatness, and they remind us that we are, after all, very small in the grand scheme of things.

The majestic, distant views are inspiring, but no more so than a mountain meadow where the noise of a rushing, snow-fed stream competes with the soft, brushing voice of the wind in the pines, where the songs of birds and the bugle of a bull elk form a chorus to God's greatness.

If the earth's oceans are the physical source of life because of the waters they hold, then the mountains are the couriers of this life source. From the mountains you can see the storms roll across the flatlands below, bringing water from the ocean and depositing it on the valleys and slopes. Silver threads in the valleys sew the highlands to other climates. These rivers and streams catch the water and carry it along the journey back to the ocean. Along the way, they bring nourishment to all kinds of life.

East River Valley, Colorado.

Fire

The valley was a picture of peace that afternoon: mule deer browsed on twigs and branches. . . sandhill cranes flew gracefully with their long necks stretched out, then landed and lurched around on bean-pole legs. . . snow geese flocked by the thousands to the fields nearby. . . the myriads of ducks almost blackened the sky when they took off from the river. . . coyotes, coons, and cougar looked for any misstep so they could have a meal, too.

Then. . . .

In the afternoon heat, a thunderhead formed to the west. Strong winds announced its arrival as it pushed east over the land. By now the sun's light was almost gone in the gray swirl of clouds overhead.

A flash of white! Before the thunder was heard, a nearby tree was struck by the lightning! Fire danced down the trunk to the ground. As the thunder crashed, hunks of flaming bark exploded off and fell into the parched grass!

Then quiet. Only a little wind. A little rain.

A few minutes later, the grass around the tree was smoking. The breeze drove the fledgling fire, and in seconds it was out of control. The dry grass was its tinder; the low limbs of trees became its fuel. Over one ridge, then another. The fire crowned, then raced downhill, only to climb the next ridge and devour another hill.

I'm sure the animals raced for their lives in front of the flames. Most of them, anyway. Smoke confused the birds, but they somehow found a way out. Older animals had seen this thing before. . . somewhere. . . sometime. They knew to run as fast as they could!

But some of them didn't understand. Or maybe they were just too scared. A raccoon climbed a tree. It had worked when other dangers threatened, but not this time. A coyote mom tried to take care of her pups, but she couldn't get them to move fast enough. She stayed with them to the end.

Everywhere. . . chaos, fear, noise, flight!

Mule deer and sandhill cranes in a field near the Rio Grande River.

The next morning, the fire was miles away. Maybe the U.S. Forest Service could put it out before it consumed too many more ridges, but it was too late for the already-charred ground. As the sun dawned, the black hulks of tree trunks stuck up from the gray ashes. Smoke still rose from thousands of smouldering fires as the last remnants of life were quickly consumed. The valley looked more like the moon than a forest and wetlands.

Rains came a few days later, and now no grasses held the waters in check. Torrents of ash mud sludged down the sides of hills and into the streams. The ground was laid bare. Empty. Dead. Barren.

A few weeks later, the first sprigs of grass sprouted. You had to look really hard to find them, but they were there. A few days more. . . a wildflower or two. Then hundreds. Then thousands. The color of the landscape changed from dull gray to a soft, rich green—with those long, ugly, black hulks of charred tree trunks still serving as sentinels.

As the bushes, seedlings, and grasses flourished in the sun's light, the animals gradually returned. In fact, the next year's growth supported far more animals than before the fire. Nature uses the hot hand of fire to sweep away all the old, upper tier foliage so new growth can flourish on the ground, and this provides the best dinner table for God's creatures.

The Lord uses the fire of suffering in our lives, too, to clean out old attitudes and perspectives. We may feel barren and empty for a while, but in their place, he brings a rich newness. Anger and bitterness become hope and forgiveness. Pride becomes tenderness. Tension turns into grace. Sometimes the flame burns long and slow. Sometimes it burns hot and is over in an instant. Either way, if we allow him, God can plant his seedlings of love, faith, and hope in our charred, barren ashes.

The writer to the Hebrews said,

> *No discipline seems pleasant at the time, but painful. Later on, however, it produces a harvest of righteousness and peace for those who have been trained by it.*
> *Hebrews 12:11*

Snow geese.

Opposite: The wetlands come to life as ducks, geese, and cranes begin a new day.

165

Foxtails and yarrow bend in a mountain meadow.

San Juan River, New Mexico.

The Gunnison River runs through the steep walls of the Black Canyon in Colorado.

This is the secret of the High Places, Grace and Glory, it is the lovely and perfect law of the whole universe.
Hannah Hurnard,
Hind's Feet on High Places

Opposite: Rocky Mountain bighorn ram.

*Snow geese head south at
the approach of winter.*

*Opposite: A cottontail
emerges from its hole to find
a world covered with snow.*

Highlands

Bighorn sheep live in some of the highest and most treacherous terrain in North America. Winter brings strong and bitter winds blasting the rocky slopes which are home for the sheep. The storms dump a thick blanket of snow on the highlands and make food difficult to find. The slippery snow also makes already-precarious footing on the rocks even more dangerous. Many sheep fall from the jagged mountains and are killed or injured.

Despite the dangers of the mountains, these heights also provide safety because very few predators venture into this domain. The sheep, though, must stay on guard. A golden eagle might swoop in to steal a lamb from the herd, and mountain lions wait in ambush for the unwary. This is not an easy life for these beautiful sheep, but it is one they were created to live.

Like the bighorn, people were created to live on the heights. The desire for power and pleasures, however, brought sin into the world. We have fallen from our high places, but we have been caught by God's hand. God sent his Son to take the blame for our selfishness, and he has given us a chance to be close to him once again.

Jesus told his disciples, "I have come that they might have life, and have it to the full" (John 10:10b). We are called to choose the right path, to be on guard against evil, and to live in a way that pleases our Maker. The abundant life has its share of dangers, but if we retain a wary, cautious eye, this life offers the greatest heights of joy, love, and peace. This is the life we are created to live.

The pictures of the Harlequin ducks and the shy cow elk were taken while Barbara and I were on our honeymoon in Canada. The beautifully marked Harlequins love the swift water of rivers. Elk are plentiful in the thick forests and high meadows of the Banff National Forest. Barbara is always very gracious and unselfish as she puts up with my interest in photography—even on our honeymoon!

Canada geese loaf on a
river.

*A mule deer buck peers
above the sagebrush.*

*Kit Carson National Forest,
New Mexico.*

Canada geese.

The Lord is my shepherd, I shall not be in want.
　　He makes me lie down in green pastures,
he leads me beside quiet waters,
　　he restores my soul.
He guides me in paths of righteousness for his
　　name's sake.

Psalm 23:1-3

Under Distant Skies

You may fly at other times low enough
to see the animals on the plains and
to feel towards them as God did when
he had just created them. . . .
Isak Dineson, *Out of Africa*

Everything about Africa seemed different from anything we had ever seen before. The skies seemed bluer, redder, whiter, more expansive. The light was brighter; the night, darker. Our expectations had been heightened by the novels we had read about this wild continent, but Africa far exceeded our expectations. Our good friends, Dave and Darian Reichert and John and Wendy Vandermeer, joined Barbara and me on this venture into a foreign culture that at times seemed surreal. Our adrenaline sharpened our appreciation of every scene, every moment, every encounter.

We were in "The Dark Continent" for only a short time, but we encountered things that we could not have experienced in our comparatively tame homeland. I wish we could have seen Africa when it was in its glory—when vast herds migrated long distances following the rains, before man's encroachment made protected parks and refuges the way of life for the splendid beasts that inhabit the land. Still, there were thrilling moments when we were on Africa's terms, when danger made our senses sharper than ever before. The sky, the trees, the waters, the land, and the beasts seemed more splendid because they were seen through wide, wondering eyes.

*Plains zebras on the
grasslands.*

Lion!" I yelled as the animal's form materialized out of the
thorny brush. My heart pounded as the cat growled his
displeasure at our presence. He stayed only a few seconds
before melting into the scenery. The thing that impressed me
the most about this animal was his size. I watched him in
awe. I felt vulnerable and small. . . very grateful for the
moment. . . and for the safety of the truck!

Perils of Africa

Football season was over, and I was going on vacation. My seventh year in the NFL was fairly successful, and I was poised to be the starting quarterback for the Houston Oilers the next season. I sat in the office of our owner, who was trying to convince me to stay and work out the details of a contract. He was concerned about investing his money in someone who might never return.

He knew I was going to Africa.

"You won't get eaten by a lion, will you, Cody?" he asked me.

I laughed as I walked out the door. I turned to look at him. He wasn't laughing.

(I looked back on his question after my eighth and final season which consisted of two separated shoulders, a broken nose, and a career-ending knee injury, and I thought it might have been a lot easier and less painful for both of us if a lion had had me for lunch!)

Africa is not the place to go if you are paralyzed by the thought of death. That continent can make even those who have faith in their eternal salvation utter the same words over and over, "Not now, Lord! I'm not ready yet!"

Our fears of Africa are enhanced by the stories we read or hear. We fear the unknown. . . and we fear what could be lurking in the tall grass (known as "adrenaline grass" for obvious reasons) or in the shadows. We hear strange sounds in the trees. We hear steps in the bushes. At least we *thought* we heard something! Our minds race back to the tales of savagery in a Capstick book. We know they are out there somewhere: the lion, the leopard, the cape buffalo. . . all waiting to pounce!

But you don't even have to set foot into the fabled African "bush" to meet an unexpected end.

We were sitting in the airport in Harare, Zimbabwe, waiting for our flight to Maun, Botswana. I looked closely at the banner hanging above the ticket counter which proudly proclaimed: "Air Zimbabwe, Number 1 Airline in Zimbabwe."

That was comforting! I had just assumed that it was the *only* airline in the country. It might have been the only airline whose planes could get off the ground. During one flight on Air Zimbabwe, we were diverted to the airstrip in the jungles of the Hwange National Park to pick up the passengers from Air Zim's other plane which was experiencing mechanical problems. As we descended, we could see a Jeep speeding down the pavement under us chasing the sable antelope and impalas from the runway!

As interesting as air travel is in Africa, travel by car is even more insane. We were run off the road twice by crazy African drivers. . . once by a car passing a bus. . . on a curve . . . in the mountains. . . at night.

We had other tense moments on our travels. We were leaving Mana Pools National Park near the Zambezi River, and we had to stop to get our vehicle sprayed for tsetse flies, a carrier of sleeping sickness which killed thousands of people in Africa not so long ago. I asked the man if the poison was harmful to humans, and he apparently didn't like my questioning his actions. He turned the vintage 1950's sprayer toward my middle and pushed the plunger! He squirted me with the liquid, glared at me, and said with a straight face, "Now you die." After a moment's pause, he broke into a toothless grin (except for the one in the corner of his mouth which gleamed in contrast to his dark skin). Then he waved us on.

Nothing in the wilds of Texas or anywhere else in the world compares to being in the African bush. There, your senses are acutely aware of the sights, smells, and sounds around you.

Tension and adrenaline can make you savor the humor and beauty in life. They are part of what makes Africa what it is. In the same way, a brush with death makes you appreciate life. It is the one sure thing that we know will happen sooner or later. Everything else that happens along the way is "iffy."

Everywhere throughout the country we were crossing were signs
that the lion was lord and that his reign was cruel.
Theodore Roosevelt, *African Game Trails*

Opposite: A zebra wears the mark of a narrow escape. The big cats are always nearby, and this zebra may not be as fortunate tomorrow. The zebra, though, isn't defenseless. Many lions and leopards have lost their lives to the devastating kicks delivered by this wild horse.

A "go away bird" (a gray lourie) watches from a tree as gemsbok, springbok, and zebra compete for the lushest grasses. The gray lourie gets its nickname from the call it makes. We heard the almost pleading cry from somewhere in the bush as if the land itself was telling us we didn't belong there: "Ga-way! Ga-way!"

With mud on his horns, a greater kudu bull travels through the bush.

A cheetah family at a water hole on the Etosha Plains. These animals were once kept by Arabs, Abyssinians, and Mongol emperors to hunt antelope on the plains. But even the fastest land animal on earth (reaching 60 mph on short bursts) can't outrun ever-encroaching sprawl of civilization. The status of this beautiful cat is threatened by overhunting, poaching, and physical weaknesses caused by inbreeding of decreased populations of cheetahs. In spite of the efforts of many to save and restore the cheetah's numbers, its future is uncertain.

The Plague

Barbara and I enjoyed our journey to Africa with our friends, Dave and Darian and John and Wendy. Dave and John had been through Africa several years before, and they scheduled our trip to include some of the sights they had enjoyed, plus some new places of interest. Our three-week trip consisted of a lot of travelling by plane, truck and canoe covering the countries of Zimbabwe and Namibia, with short stops at the airport in Maun, Botswana. The many, long hours of travel—combined with too few hours of sleep—brought out a few cases of nerves and impatience. But all in all, it was an awesome experience! With one exception: the night of the plague.

The trip from Etosha Pan in northern Namibia to the desert region near Sossusvlei in southwest Namibia had taken most of two days. Except for an overnight stay in the coastal town of Swakopmund and a stop in Damaraland for a scary lunch of fried egg sandwiches, the two days were spent en route over dirt roads on the edge of the Namib Desert. We were tired and hungry as we pulled into a gas station, which was conveniently located for our travels: it was stuck in the middle of nowhere! We filled the tanks on both of the small, four-wheel drive trucks that had taken us and our gear over miles of desolate terrain.

Because the light was fading fast, we decided we shouldn't travel any further into the desert that day. We entered the store and found the owner feeding crickets to several large, black scorpions in a glass aquarium on the counter. The man continued to feed his pets. He was obviously pleased by their vicious competition over the morsels as he told us the details of the ugly insect's poisonous sting. The man was large, and he had the appearance of someone who would be considered "back woods," except there weren't any woods anywhere near the place. In a German accent common to the region, he asked if we were planning to venture on. When we replied that we hadn't decided, he suggested a place to camp. We paid him for the gas and thanked him for his advice. We walked outside into the falling darkness and got into the trucks. As we pulled out of the station, we saw a hulking shape leave the store and get into an old pickup with only one headlight.

We found the small rest area the man had suggested as a campground. It seemed as misplaced as the gas station. And as deserted. We hadn't seen another traveler in over ten hours. We set up the rented tents, unpacked our necessities, and began preparing dinner on a campfire we built between the dead, barren trees that sheltered the rest area. We snacked on cheese and crackers and drank sodas as we watched the steaks sizzling on the grill. Softly, the leaves on the trees began to rattle in a breeze. But we couldn't feel any wind. . . .

In the darkness, Dave wondered out loud, "I don't remember any leaves on these trees." Suddenly he yelled and threw his bottled drink high in the air! He grabbed his arm. Just then, the bottle broke on the hard ground. We turned our flashlights toward Dave. Before we could ask for an explanation, strange objects hurtled at the lights in our hands!

Darian was slicing cheese with a long-bladed knife when one of the things hit her on the head. She jerked her hand toward it, narrowly missing her scalp with the knife blade! We gasped in unison, then trained our flashlights at her feet. In the spotlight, we saw an enormous, four-inch grasshopper! Darian looked at the creature, put down her knife. Without saying a single word, she walked to one of the tents and went to sleep.

When we realized these varmints were coming to the light, we turned off the flashlights. Our skin crawled as we listened to the noise of hundreds—or thousands!—or millions!—of monstrous grasshoppers in the trees only a few feet above us! Other marauders took aim at our campfire. . . and at us, too! These Old Testament villains hit us with sharp blows and clung to our skin and clothes with their clawed feet. As quickly as we could, we stomped out the fire.

After an eternity—or a few minutes (depending if you were actually there or not!)—we sat in total darkness eating our rare steaks. The "leaves" stopped shaking and silence set in. After we regained our composure, we laughed at ourselves.

In the darkness, the only light we saw was the lone headlight that passed slowly on the road several times during the night. Maybe the man from the gas station was checking on us to make sure we were okay. Maybe not. I didn't trust him, so I stood watch by the tents with a hatchet.

Several hours crept by. No sounds. No headlight. I finally released my death-grip on the hatchet, gave up my guard post, and crawled into the tent. Morning came early, but not too soon for any of us.

Camping in the desert. Great idea!

A pale, chanting goshawk perched in front of a fiery sunset.

Alone. A gemsbok treks across the harsh climate of the Namib Desert in a continuing search for life-sustaining food and water.

The Namib Desert is a thin strip of Atlantic shoreline that runs nearly the entire length of Namibia. This desolate stretch is one of the wildest places on earth, and it has some of the largest sand dunes on the planet. The dunes closest to the sea travel as far as 50 feet in a single year as they are driven by the strong, ocean winds. The Namib is also one of the driest places on the globe, receiving an average of less than an inch of rain a year.

A surprising number of creatures live in this seemingly inhospitable place. Gemsbok and springbok, and even elephants, traverse the enormous dunes in search of food that provides the moisture they need to survive. Other creatures drink the moisture that condenses on their own bodies at night. A dense fog forms every evening on the ocean and spreads inland, providing this moisture for the wildlife. The sidewinder viper buries itself in the sand to wait for prey and to escape the mid-day heat. At night it reappears on the surface of the sands. In the relative cool of the early morning hours, the snake runs its forked tongue over its coils to drink the droplets of condensed water. At the same time of morning, the darkling beetle stands on its head to allow drops to roll down its body into its mouth.

But the fog also keeps the region unsettled by people because it severely lowers visibility and prevents access to the Namib by sea. This area is called "The Skeleton Coast" because of the remains of ships littering the shoreline. These wrecks serve as a reminder of vain attempts to civilize this land. People have stayed away from this forbidding desert, leaving it to the creatures which have adapted to its harsh climate.

Zebras rest on the plains.

Opposite: Born with stripes as unique to it as fingerprints are to humans, a zebra colt stands on wobbly legs in a dangerous new world. The stripes create an optical illusion to predators, allowing the zebra to blend with the patterns of grass and brush in the African landscape.

A hippopotamus (Greek for "river horse") in a territorial display on the Zambezi River. The hippo has killed more people in Africa than all the lions, elephants, and cape buffalo combined.

A View from the River

The Ruckomechi Camp stands on the banks of the Zambezi River as it flows through Mana Pools National Park on the northern boundary of Zimbabwe. Our stay there produced some of the most exhilarating sights and feelings we experienced. Our drive through Mana Pools en route to the camp was interrupted as we made the last bend in the rough road. Only a hundred yards from the camp, we saw a pack of cape hunting dogs engaged in a wild and bloody orgy over an impala they had killed.

Over dinner that night, we told the guides and guests about the scene of carnage. The camp guides told us what we had seen was, indeed, a rare sight since the wild dogs weren't numerous in that area. Our excitement grew as we listened to the accounts of the events that had taken place on the river in recent months. During the week prior to our arrival, a Zambian fisherman was killed by a hippo across the river from the camp. A few months earlier, a man lost his arm to a crocodile as he rescued his son from its jaws. And before that, a lion mauled a man as he slept on the bank after a day canoeing down the river.

Later that night we lay under our mosquito net and listened to the muffled roars of a lion (the same one?) prowling around the camp. The beast's groans seemed to be only a few feet from the thatched-roofed hut, and at that moment, a thatch-roofed hut didn't seem like a lot of protection! The lion spent a few hours searching for something—or someone—as it padded through the group of huts. The groans stopped at some point in the night, and sleep finally fell on the camp once more. . . but only for a short while. The heavy steps and bellowing laughter of hippos woke us and reminded us of our voyage on the river the next day.

Several people warned us not to take the trip down the river. Each one had his own story of horror similar to those the guides recounted that first evening. The guides were simply allowing us to make a decision, whether to take the trip or not, based on the facts. The doomsayers tried to prevent us from playing the main characters in one of the oft-told stories of peril on the river. Nonetheless, there we were early the next morning, listening to the safety procedures from our guide, Alan. I couldn't remember listening to the advice of coaches, parents, or teachers with the same rapt attention I gave Alan at that moment!

We rode in land cruisers to a drop point a few miles up the Zambezi. The plan was for us to reach camp before dark. After Alan repeated the instructions to our satisfaction (again), we decided that if we didn't make it back, we would at least have a thrilling story of our demise to recall when we were reunited in heaven. As we eased the light aluminum boats into the water, the demented, bellowing of the rotund river horses rolled to our ears from around the bend.

Alan had explained that the hippos were very territorial. Most accidents occurred when the huge beasts were surprised and cut off from their deep water sanctuaries. Hippos weigh up to 7000 pounds, can open their jaws 150 degrees wide, and have razor-sharp lower canines as long as twenty inches. To avoid surprising them, we let the hippos know of our presence by beating our paddles on the water each time we saw a pod of them or approached a turn in the river. We passed through the upper stretch of the journey and watched some hippos submerge upon our approach. Others gave half-hearted protests of our intrusion with gaping jaws and flashing teeth, and a few of these mammoth beasts absent-mindedly flicked their ears and quietly eyed our passing. We couldn't help but admire these huge, dangerous animals. As we made the halfway point, a crocodile slipped from a sand bar into the deep channel that lay in front of us.

Alan led us to the sand bar for a break, and after a dip in the shallow water on the opposite side of the sandy island from the croc, we listened to Alan's tale of growing up in Zimbabwe. We heard about his love for this land and its people. He spoke with respect for the animals. On one occasion when Alan was a boy, he found himself face-to-face

Here, upon the roof of Africa,
wandered the heavy, wise, majestic
bearer of the ivory. He was deep in
his own thoughts and wanted to be
left to himself.
  —from *Out of Africa*

with a cape buffalo. Alan escaped being gored and trampled by climbing into a deep, steep crevasse, but the buffalo kept an all-night vigil over him. Our fearless guide also voiced a deep appreciation for the freedom that was won in the bloody war for independence a decade before. He talked about his hope for continued progress in the relationships of blacks and whites as they leave their bitter, war-scarred past and build a new Zimbabwe. He spoke of his pride in his country and his desire to share its treasures by becoming the first certified black guide in Zimbabwe.

Soon we resumed our strokes and witnessed the life of the river around the next bend. With a new appreciation, we paddled past lush vegetation, colorful birds, and fascinating land and water beasts. Then Alan veered sharply toward the bank and motioned for us to follow. We travelled as close as we could get to the juts and dips of the shoreline for a hundred yards or so. I saw Barbara riding in the first canoe with Alan. She raised her camera and pointed it at something out of my view. Dave and I rounded a bushy point and saw eight giant, bull elephants at the water's edge only twenty feet from Barbara! They trumpeted a warning and turned to escape the strangers who had caught them unaware. There wasn't enough room for all of them to climb the trail that was carved into the bluff. They pushed each other in frustration. Suddenly they panicked! The elephants turned and charged! They stopped at the edge of the deep channel, kicked the dirt, and flapped their huge ears. They sounded their agitation once more, then turned and clamored their way up the bluff and out of sight. We sat breathless in our flimsy canoes.

As the sky turned orange, we made the last turn of our journey and recognized the dim lights of camp. Our paddle strokes slowed as we drank in the final minutes of the wonderful day. The peace was broken by an enormous explosion of water behind Dave! We turned to see the monstrous head of a hippo ten feet from John and Wendy! We glided by, hoping he wasn't too startled. . . or too angry! He slowly submerged into the dark waters, but before he was gone, he said good-bye in that now-familiar bellowing laugh.

Barbara and I lay under the mosquito net that night and talked of how we had never felt so alive. A part of us wished we could stay. . . . And a part of us never left that river.

Waterbuck near the Zambezi River.

Emerald spotted dove.

The Mission

Amazing grace, how sweet the sound that saved a wretch like me.
I once was lost, but now I'm found, was blind but now I see.

That song came drifting down from the hills surrounding old Mutare Mission. We recognized the melody, but the words were a strange dialect. The beat had a different flair, and the joy came from a rich, full heart. The heart of Africa.

On our trip, this mission is the one place that gave us the most peace—and the most unrest. It was both comforting and uncomfortable. All six of us slept on the tile floor in one room of a cottage. We bathed each night in four inches of water. If you were first in line, you had a pretty good chance of getting clean, but if you got the last shot at the tub, well. . . maybe tomorrow.

The seats of the church pews were too shallow for a big guy, and somehow the wood became much harder toward the end of the three hour Easter service. But physical pain was nothing compared to the pain in my heart.

The mission's orphans were housed in a separate building on the grounds of the compound. Most of these children were too young to speak—and surely too young to understand why they were abandoned or why their parents had died of AIDS or some other tragedy. The only adults they had known were the occasional visitors like us and the missionaries and nurses who tirelessly cared for them. We affectionately called these little ones "the porridge kids" because they wore a grits-like layer of food, known as *sadza*, on their faces and hands. These dear children couldn't fathom worldly riches or great purposes in life. They didn't want—or expect— a lot, only love and affection. Especially Eymon.

Eymon was the oldest of the children, about four years-old, and the only one we heard speak a word. Before he leaped into the arms of anyone who would hug him, he uttered something we interpreted as "Hey, man!" I don't know if he had a given name, and I don't know if we correctly understood what he was saying in mid-jump, but I'm sure of the lesson he and the others sent with us at the moment we walked away from the orphanage. When we heard the familiar and faint sound, "Ey, mon," we turned to see the outstretched hands of the children.

Jesus said, "Whoever receives one little child like this in my name receives me" (Matthew 18:5). When I think of that orphanage, I feel a little uncomfortable. The loving labor of the nurses and missionaries invades my conscience and tells me I should do more to help. I remember the joy on the faces of the cast-off children when we hugged them, and I recall the enthusiasm in the songs the older children sang for us. It makes me feel guilty for worrying about such trivial things in my own life, but it also comforts me to realize these children have a God who loves them enough to send a Savior to them.

Even the tallest animal on earth, the giraffe, seems small under the African sky.

Praise the Lord from the earth,
    you great sea creatures and all ocean
    depths,
lightning and hail, snow and clouds,
    stormy winds that do his bidding,
you mountains and all hills,
    fruit trees and all cedars.
Wild animals and all cattle,
    small creatures and flying birds,
kings of the earth and all nations,
    you princes and all rulers on earth,
young men and maidens,
    old men and children.

Let them praise the name of the Lord,
    for his name alone is exalted;
    his splendor is above the earth and the
    heavens.
He has raised up for his people a horn,
    the praise of all his saints,
    of Israel, the people close to his heart.

Praise the Lord.
                    Psalm 148:7-14

Into the Light

I have come into the world as a light, so that
no one who believes in me should stay in darkness.
John 12:46

Why did God create things as they are? Why did he give the lion a roar, the whale a spout, and the kangaroo a pouch? Why were we created in his image? There are many mysteries of God's creation. They intrigue us. We explore and research all we possibly can, but because we don't think like God thinks, we will not—we *cannot*—completely understand his plan. We don't know why God created the universe the way he did, but we know his reason. He created it to reveal his love. God didn't *need* to create it. He *chose* to create it so he could share his love with something. . . with someone. You and me.

God teaches us about his love and majesty through the wonders of nature. He shows us love by giving us dominion over these wonders, and in return, he expects us to rule this realm with the respect it deserves. But our role in his plan extends beyond protecting the wilderness areas. Our biggest responsibility is to take care of our hearts. He commands us to love our neighbor as we love ourselves—without exception, without regard to status, nationality, or skin color. He commands us to love him with all our heart, mind, and strength. Because he gave us the wonders of the universe, including our own lives, he is worthy of nothing less.

Far too often we choose to do what we want instead of what we should. We glorify ourselves instead of glorifying him. But even then, God continues to give. In return for our sins, he gave us what we don't deserve. . . love—love that was sent to give light in the darkness.

Jesus told his disciples, "I am the way, the truth, and the life. No one comes to the Father except through me" (John 14:6). Jesus came so we could, by accepting God's love and grace, walk in eternal light.

Then I heard every creature in heaven and on earth
and under the earth and on the sea, and all that is in
them, singing:
"To him who sits on the throne and to the Lamb
be praise and honor forever and ever!"
Revelation 5:13